Flynn's Strange Win

Pamela Graham

Illustrated by Mini Goss

Momentum
Flynn's Strange Win

First published in Great Britain in 1999 by

Folens Publishers
Albert House
Apex Business Centre
Boscombe Road
Dunstable
Beds LU5 4RL

© 1999 Momentum developed by Barrie Publishing Pty Limited
Suite 513, 89 High St, Kew, Vic 3101, Australia

Pamela Graham hereby asserts her moral right to be identified as the author of this work in accordance with the Copyright, Designs and Patents Act 1988.
© 1999 Folens Ltd. on behalf of the author.
Illustrations copyright Mini Goss.

All rights reserved. No part of this publication may be reproduced or transmitted in any form or by any means, electronic or mechanical, including photocopying, recording or any information storage and retrieval system, without written permission from the publisher.

British Library Cataloguing in Publication Data.
A Catalogue record for this book is available from the British Library

ISBN 1 86202 734 X

Designed by Pauline McClenahan
Printed in Singapore by PH Productions Pte Ltd

Contents

Chapter One	A Pet Competition	5
Chapter Two	Finding a Pet	7
Chapter Three	Flynn's Pet Crab	11
Chapter Four	The Clever Pelican	13
Chapter Five	Hoppy Comes Home	17
Chapter Six	An Unusual Pet	21

Chapter One

A Pet Competition

Flynn and his friends read the sign outside the hall. "There's going to be a fair," he said, "with rides and everything."

F a i r
Saturday, March 21
Stalls and Rides!
Food and Drinks! Pet competition: biggest pet, smallest pet, prettiest pet,
ugliest pet, most unusual pet.

"A pet competition." Kara smiled. "My Fifi will be the prettiest." Her fleecy poodle bounced around her legs. "I'll put a green velvet ribbon in her hair and I'll paint her nails a gorgeous pink."

"I'll enter my mouse in the 'smallest pet' section," said Rob. "Nothing will be smaller than my mouse."

"My goldfish is," said Maria. "It's much smaller than a mouse."

Flynn didn't say anything. He kicked at the ground with the toe of his shoe. He didn't have a pet. He'd like to have a dog, but his mother was allergic to animals.

He left the others talking and made his way home. He took off his shoes and went the long way, wandering through the dunes near the beach. He stared at the sand as he walked.

What sort of pet could he find before next Saturday?

Chapter Two

Finding a Pet

When Flynn reached Shell Cove, the tide was low. He crossed the isolated mud-flats and climbed the rocks that surrounded the cove. Maybe there would be some shrimps hiding there. No one else would have a shrimp. He trod carefully, trying not to make any noise but he found nothing. He turned over bits of driftwood, but still found nothing.

As he walked back, something scuttled across the mud. Then it disappeared. He saw another one, and another. They were little crabs, darting in and out of their holes.

Maybe a crab would make a suitable pet. Flynn snatched at one. He missed. He tried again — and again. Finally, he got one. He picked it up, but it nipped his thumb. "Ow!" Flynn shook his hand. The crab fell to the ground and raced into a hole.

Then he saw one lying in the mud on the other side of a rotting log. Before he reached it, a big pelican grabbed it.

"Shoo! Get away!" shouted Flynn. He'd never seen a pelican eat a crab before. "Shoo!" The pelican couldn't move properly. He hopped a few paces and flapped his big wings.

Flynn saw that the bird was injured. Some old fishing line was knotted around his leg. The line looked as if it had been there for a long time. It was stuck firmly in the skin, and the leg was crooked.

Other pelicans dived and caught some fish. The one with the sore leg tried a couple of times but didn't catch anything.

Flynn turned away from the lively pelicans. He found another crab. This time, he didn't try to hold it. He pushed it quickly into his shoe and stuffed his sock behind it. "Got you," he shouted.

He hurried home with the crab still in his shoe. First of all, he would have to find something to keep it in. It couldn't stay in his shoe for very long.

He left his shoe with his sock in it on the porch. "You stay there," he said to the crab, even though he couldn't see it. "I'll find something to use as a home for you." He hurried into the laundry to look for a box or a bucket.

Just as he picked up a plastic bucket, he heard his mother call, "Flynn! What is this muddy shoe doing on the ... Aarrgh!"

Chapter Three

Flynn's Pet Crab

Flynn still had the bucket in his hand when he ran to the porch.

His mother was dancing from one foot to the other. The sock lay on the floor. "There was something in your shoe," she gasped. "It ran onto my foot and bit me."

"Oh, no," said Flynn. He fell to his knees and crawled around, looking for his crab.

"Don't worry about it," said his mother. "Look at my foot."

"It was my pet crab," said Flynn.

His mother stopped hopping around and stared at him. "A pet crab?" she said. "Flynn, you can't keep a crab. Crabs need to be near the water."

"There it is!" shouted Flynn. "In the corner." He rushed at the crab and quickly flicked it into the bucket. Then he looked at his mother. "I could pour some water into the bucket."

His mother shook her head. "Crabs need seawater. They have to be able to run around."

Flynn's shoulders dropped. He peered at the little crab in the bottom of the bucket. It tried to climb out, but its claws continually slipped on the smooth plastic. "I'll take you back to the mud-flats," he said sadly.

His mother smiled. "It will be happier there," she said quietly. Flynn trudged all the way back to Shell Cove. He tipped the crab out of the bucket. It scuttled over the mud and into a hole.

There goes my chance at having a pet, thought Flynn.

The pelican with the sore leg was still nearby.

Flynn picked up the bucket and began to walk home. He trailed his toes in the mud. That was when he saw the two funny little snails.

Chapter Four

The Clever Pelican

Flynn bent down to look at them. They were almost hidden under the mud. They were easy to catch. He washed the mud off them and popped them into his bucket. Snails didn't need to run around like crabs did. They would make great pets.

He hurried home with his snails. He was really pleased with them. He showed them to his mother. "They'll need food, won't they?" he asked.

His mother nodded. "They eat tiny things in the mud. Perhaps you should have brought some mud back with them."

Flynn raced back to the cove again. The tide had come in a bit, but there was still plenty of mud. He scooped some up for his two little snails.

The pelican with the sore leg hopped along the shore.

"Hello, Hoppy," whispered Flynn. Hoppy was catching crabs again. It seemed easier for this pelican to catch crabs than fish. He just stood still and waited for the crabs to come close. Then he instantly snatched them up.

"What a clever pelican," whispered Flynn. "You've taught yourself to catch something other than fish for your dinner." He managed to grab a crab and then threw it to Hoppy. The pelican caught it easily in his huge beak. Flynn watched him for a while and then set off home with his snails in their mud.

Flynn passed Kara's house and saw her washing Fifi with 'Lovable Bubbles' pet shampoo. Bubbles gently floated everywhere.

"What have you got there?" she asked.

Flynn lifted the container lid. Kara wrinkled her nose and screwed up her eyes. "Oh! It smells awful." She laughed.

Flynn grinned. "It's my special unusual pet."

"I can't see anything but a blob of mud."

"It's a surprise," said Flynn.

Rob came running up the street. "Hey! Guess what! My mouse is going to have babies. Now I'll have something smaller than Maria's goldfish."

The word 'fish' reminded Flynn of Hoppy. He looked at Fifi. She didn't have to worry about where her next meal came from.

Chapter Five

Hoppy Comes Home

Flynn played with his snails the next afternoon. He watched them move through the mud to get their food. They moved so slowly. They made him think about Hoppy again.

He went into the kitchen. "Could I have a bit of the leftover meatloaf, please?" he asked his mother. She cut him a thick slice.

Flynn put the meatloaf in a plastic container and jogged to Shell Cove.

Hoppy stood in the mud-flats, waiting for little crabs to run past him. Flynn tossed pieces of meatloaf to the lonely pelican. He caught them all. Hoppy came closer and stared at the container. He seemed to ask for more.

Flynn went to the cove every afternoon to feed Hoppy. He tried to look at the pelican's sore leg, but Hoppy wouldn't let him touch it. On Friday afternoon, Hoppy followed Flynn all the way home. Hopping and flapping, he came right up to the back door.

"Make sure he doesn't come into the house," said his mother.

Flynn gave Hoppy some more food, and the large bird settled down beside the door. He was still there the next morning. He followed Flynn into the back garden and watched him get ready for the pet competition. First, Flynn washed his snails. Then he washed the container and put leaves in the bottom of it. The snails looked better sitting on clean leaves rather than on a patch of mud.

When it was time to go to the hall, Hoppy wanted to follow. "Shoo! Stay home!" said Flynn. "You can't come. This is for pets, not wild animals." Hoppy flapped backward, and Flynn marched down the street with his snails in their plastic container.

He met his friends on the way. Rob's mouse snuggled into some shredded paper in a little cardboard box. Beside her were four tiny pink mice.

Maria carried a bowl with one shiny goldfish in it. She peered at the baby mice. "Those baby ones don't count," she said. "When they grow up they'll be bigger than my goldfish."

Fifi trotted next to Kara. Her gorgeous pink nails clicked on the concrete. She had a green velvet ribbon on her head and a red collar around her neck. "What's your surprise?" Kara asked Flynn. "Can we see what's in your container now?"

His friends crowded around as Flynn carefully pulled back the lid of the container.

Chapter Six

An Unusual Pet

"I've got two special snails," said Flynn proudly. "They're called Swifty and Speedy. They're really great pets."

"How are they great pets?" asked Kara.

"Well, you always know where they are. They're not fast enough to run away. And they're not noisy."

"They're certainly different," said Rob.

They all walked to the spacious hall where the school headteacher was in charge of the pet competition. "All pets over here," he called through a loudspeaker.

Kids came from everywhere. There were cats and canaries, dogs and ducks, lizards and lovebirds.

"There's nothing smaller than my goldfish," said Maria.

"My baby mice are," Rob gloated.

"All line up now," said the headteacher. "Our judge is the local vet. She will speak to each of you and ask about your pet."

Suddenly, a boy ran up carrying an ant farm under his arm. "Oh, no!" said Maria and Rob together.

A cat came too close to Fifi. She barked and struggled. Kara pulled tightly on the lead. Flynn put his container on the ground so he could help Kara. A girl came and took the cat away, but Fifi's green bow had fallen off. Her collar was twisted and she wouldn't stand still.

The vet moved along the line and spoke to Rob and then to Maria and wrote in her notebook. She looked at Fifi and wrote hurriedly in her notebook again. Then she stopped in front of Flynn. He was last in the line. "And what category is your pet in?" she asked.

Flynn picked up his container. "The most unusual," he said. He looked into the container, and his jaw dropped.

It was empty!

The vet glanced behind Flynn's legs. "Well, I agree. A one-legged pelican really is a most unusual pet." Flynn turned and saw Hoppy swallow something.

The vet smiled and firmly shook Flynn's hand. "Congratulations! You've won first prize!"

She bent down and looked at Hoppy's leg. "Come and see me later and I'll try to fix his leg."

"A pelican!" said Rob.

"You didn't tell us you had a pelican," said Kara.

"What a wonderful pet!" said Maria.

"Yes, he is, isn't he?" grinned Flynn. And Hoppy let him stroke the back of his long neck.